Designer Malcolm Smythe
Art Director Charles Matheson
Series Editor James McCarter
Editor Cecilia Weston-Baker
Consultant Charles Messenger
Researcher John MacClancy

Illustrators Rob Shone
Andy Farmer

Designed and produced by
Aladdin Books Ltd
70 Old Compton Street
London W1

Printed in Belgium

*First published in the
United States in* 1985 *by*
Franklin Watts
387 Park Avenue South
New York NY 10016

ISBN 531 04935 3

Library of Congress
Catalog Card No. 84-51814

For the purposes of this book:
The tonnage of ships is conventionally described in long tons.
One long ton equals 1.016 tonnes, or 2240 lbs.

*The publishers would like to thank the following organizations
and individuals for their help in the preparation of this book:*
The Australian Department of Defence; Boeing Marine Systems;
British Shipbuilders; DAVA; Ingalls Shipbuilders; Military Archives
Research Services; The Royal Navy Public Relations Office;
F. Spooner; Todd Pacific Shipyards; The US Navy Public Relations
Office; Vosper Thorneycroft Ltd.

Photographic Credits:
4/5 Royal Navy (RN); 8/9 US Navy, DAVA; 10/11 US Navy; 12/13
US Navy; 14/15 DAVA; 16/17 DAVA; 18/19 US Navy; 20/21
F. Spooner, US Navy, RN; 22/23 Vosper Thorneycroft, DAVA,
F. Spooner, RN, Ministry of Defence; 24/25 RN; 26/27 RN, US
Navy, TASS; 28/29 Australian Department of Defence, RN,
DAVA; 30/31 US Navy; 32 US Navy; 34 to 44 Military Archives
Research Services, The MacClancy Collection, The Robert Hunt
Library, Ingalls Shipbuilders, DAVA.

20th CENTURY WEAPONS

SURFACE WARSHIPS

ROBERT VAN TOL

FRANKLIN WATTS

New York · London · Toronto · Sydney

Introduction

Warships are the single most complex machines built for war. This is partly because they are the largest. The biggest carrier has a displacement of 95,900 tonnes (94,400 tons) and a crew of over 6000 compared to the largest aircraft which is under 355 tonnes (350 tons), with 360 crew and passengers, and tanks, which are all under 71 tonnes (70 tons) with a normal crew of four. But the main reason is that a warship is expected to fight in three quite different areas.

The fighting warship
The warship is expected to be able to defend itself, and any ships it may be escorting, from air attack. This means that it must be equipped with sophisticated sensors, to search the horizon at long range, for attacking aircraft and missiles; and a variety of weapons, to try and shoot these down as they approach the ship.

Secondly, the ship is expected to defend itself from, and to be able to attack, other warships. This means that it must be able to scan the surface of the sea for other vessels, classify those found as being either friendly, neutral or enemy, and either attack or avoid the enemy warships. Thirdly, the warship must be able to defend itself from enemy submarines hiding in the ocean's depths. This is a particularly difficult role, demanding sophisticated underwater sensors, patience during the long hunts and skill in finally locating and attacking the enemy underwater.

An expensive vessel
The sensors and weapons for these three quite different areas of war must all be crammed into a single ship which also contains its engines, and the normal sailing features to operate the ship. It must also have space for the living quarters for the crew and for the command center. It is from here that the ship's actions and movements can be coordinated with that of the whole fleet.

This makes warships complicated and costly. The general trend is that fewer warships are built each year because each year they become more expensive, as they are made more complex. This is not to say that warships are any less important. Both the US and the USSR are spending a great deal of money on warships because they allow these superpowers to send their military power to almost any part of the world that they are needed, especially to allow their forces to await off-shore.

Contents

Above: HMS Glamorgan fires Sea Slug missile

Anatomy of a Surface Warship

Warships are very compact in design. All available space is used to keep the size and the cost of the vessel down. This is often quite apparent because of the amount of clutter on the outside of the warship – the mass of missile launchers, radar and radio antennae, funnels, masts, guns and small boats. However, some navies, in particular the US Navy, try to make the decks (or topsides) of their ships look as uncluttered as possible. But, whatever the outside appearance, the inside is always cramped.

Space on the top decks of a warship is always important. It is here that almost all of the ship's weapons and sensors are located, in addition to all the normal ship's equipment stored there. This includes gear for mooring and anchoring the ship when it is in port. These are located at the bow of the ship. Behind the bow is the forecastle (pronounced "folk's!"), where some of the main weapons are positioned. The forecastle must be high enough above the water so that in heavy seas the ship is not swamped by waves. If it is not high enough, not only will the bridge be sprayed with water (obscuring vision) but in heavy seas the ship will often slam into the next wave immediately after passing through the first. This is a very unpleasant feeling and makes the ship very difficult to operate. The bridge is behind the forecastle and it is traditionally from here that the ship is sailed.

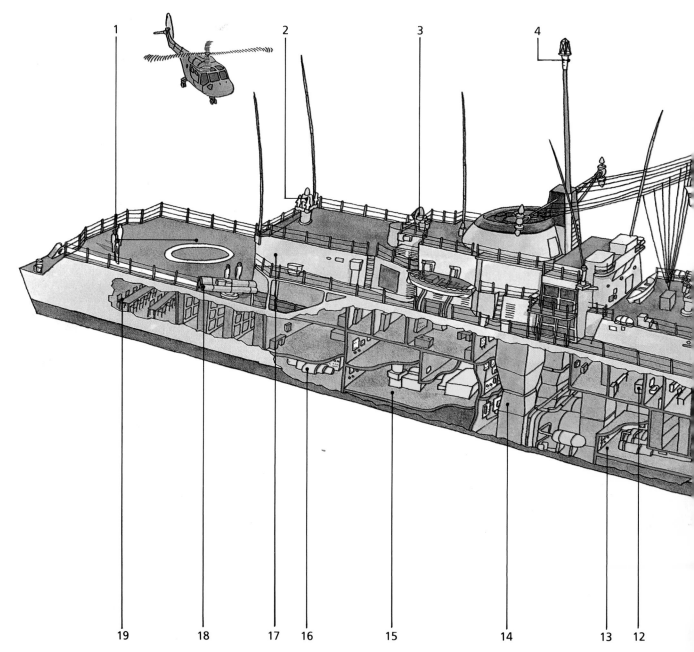

It is mounted high up with a good view over the bow and sides of the ship. Behind the bridge, on most ships, is a mast on which is mounted various radio aerials and navigation, search and fire control radar. The highest radar on the mast is normally the search radar, since from here it has the best unobstructed view of the horizon. Behind the mast is an area normally used for the ship's small boats, used in port; the funnel to expel the engine's exhaust gases and normally a second mast with more radar, radio and other electronic devices.

The Stern
Further back, at the stern of the ship, is the quarterdeck, which like the forecastle, is normally clear deck used for weapons and, if carried, the ship's helicopter. Also at the stern will be the machinery for the towed sonars (if carried). This layout of the upper deck varies slightly among individual designs, but all these elements will generally be present in most warships. For example, nuclear-powered ships do not need a funnel, while others may have several funnels or the funnels may be combined with the mast.

Weapons
The sorts of weapons carried will vary depending on the mission the ship is expected to carry out but generally it will have the following: a helicopter landing pad, often with a hangar to store the helicopter; an air defense missile system, often supplemented by a gun air defense system; some anti-ship missiles, a medium caliber gun (between 76 and 152mm (3-6 in); some torpedo tubes for anti-submarine torpedoes and a rocket launcher which fires decoys to guide an attacking missile away from the ship. Inside the ship are the engines, the command center, and the living quarters for the crew. The computers and electronic equipment, the radios and weapons systems plus the magazines which load the gun as well as some of the missile systems, also have to be incorporated into the ship.

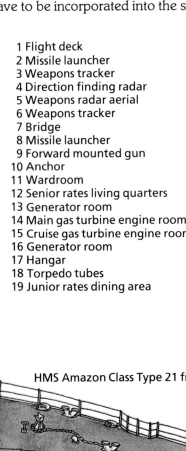

1 Flight deck
2 Missile launcher
3 Weapons tracker
4 Direction finding radar
5 Weapons radar aerial
6 Weapons tracker
7 Bridge
8 Missile launcher
9 Forward mounted gun
10 Anchor
11 Wardroom
12 Senior rates living quarters
13 Generator room
14 Main gas turbine engine room
15 Cruise gas turbine engine room
16 Generator room
17 Hangar
18 Torpedo tubes
19 Junior rates dining area

HMS Amazon Class Type 21 frigate

The Machinery

There are many different types of ship's engine. They range from a 1016 tonne (1000 ton) landing craft's 225hp diesel up to the two nuclear reactors, developing 280,000hp, used to power the large US 97,550 tonne (96,000 ton) aircraft carriers.

The carrier's reactors drive the massive ship through four steam turbines which turn four propellers, giving a maximum speed of over 30 knots, and also provide the ship with all the other power that it needs. Steam power is used for the four catapults which can drive a 15.2 tonne (15 ton) aircraft from 0 to over 160kph (100 mph) in 90m (295 ft). Electrical power is needed for the radar, radio sets, lighting, air conditioning, heating, computers and kitchen. Moreover, the reactors can provide power for about 13 years before refueling. Nuclear power is, however, expensive and really only worthwhile in large ships. Most warships have either steam turbine, gas turbine or diesel engines, or a combination of these.

Combined engine systems

Each type of engine is useful in different ways. The steam turbine gives good overall performance for the amount of power it produces and the amount of fuel it uses. Gas turbines, developed using aircraft engine technology, have very good high-power performance. In particular, they can reach maximum power very quickly, but tend to use a lot of fuel when not running at maximum power. Diesels are particularly good at running at moderate power levels while not using too much fuel. Thus a typical ship might have a COmbined Diesel Or Gas (CODOG) system in which there is a set of diesel engines for economical cruising, and another of gas turbines for high speed sprints. The problem is that the ship has to use two types of fuel. One way of getting over this is to use, as modern Dutch and British warships do, small 4250 hp gas turbines for cruising and two large 28,000 hp gas turbines for maximum speed. Yet this is still quite complex since it involves maintaining two different types of engine. Many US ships run on one large 20,000 hp gas turbine when cruising and turn on the others (normally four in all) for high speed, accepting the higher fuel consumption in favor of simpler operation.

Power and performance

It should be remembered that traveling as fast as possible is not as important as it once was. Most ships cannot go faster than 30 to 40 knots because, beyond these speeds, the extra power exerted is cancelled out by the extra drag from the hull caused by going faster. So it needs a massive increase in power for a small increase in speed; an expensive investment for little return. In any case, there is little to be gained given the speed of the modern submarine, not to mention aircraft and missiles. What is important is that the ship can travel economically so that it does not have to be refueled too often. It must also run quietly so that the engines' noise does not give it away and that the ship can sprint; so that it can do fast twists and turns when trying to avoid attacks from aircraft and missiles. Of these three, quietness is the most difficult to achieve. It is the vibrations of the engines which make the most noise. To minimize this, the engines of modern ships are mounted on rafts suspended on springs, so that as much vibration as possible is absorbed.

US nuclear-powered guided missile cruisers

USSR Krivak class destroyer, Bodry

Power control

Controlling the power output of a series of engines, which can produce the same amount of power as a small power station, is a sensitive task. The Chief Engineer must be ready to provide the ship's Captain with maximum speed, best cruising speed or quietest possible engine running, as needed. This requires constant monitoring of the engines' performance, and ensuring that worn out parts are replaced. Thus, each engine has its own monitoring panel which reports to the main engine room console, which in turn reports to a console in the Combat Information Center, which keeps the Captain of the ship informed.

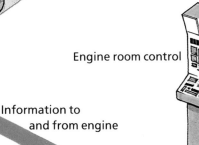

Information to and from bridge

Main engine control

Bridge control

Propellers

Engine room control

Information to and from engine

Two gas turbine engines and gearboxes

Recognition of engine types

The type of engines used by a ship can normally be determined by the type of its funnel. Large ships with no funnel are usually nuclear-powered because nuclear power does not produce any exhaust fumes which need to be expelled from the ship. Gas turbine ships tend to have large funnels, mounted high, because they produce large amounts of exhaust which is very hot. These need to be placed away from the ship's electronics. Diesel engine funnels are a lot smaller and can often be incorporated into the ship's mast.

Monitoring engine room controls, USS New Jersey

Surface Warfare

The two most dangerous adversaries to surface warships in naval warfare are aircraft and submarines, and warships spend most of their time and effort defending themselves and those that they are escorting from air and sub-surface attacks. However, to the incautious commander, warships themselves can inflict considerable damage alone, especially with the new range of anti-ship cruise missiles. Fighting against other warships is known as Surface Warfare. It is a skill which must not be neglected. One important element of surface warfare is the anti-ship missile (ASM).

Although Germany employed a limited number of crude but effective anti-ship missiles in World War II, it was the Russians who first developed large numbers of anti-ship missiles. These could be launched either from bomber aircraft, from submarines or from warships. Some anti-ship missiles had very long ranges, such as the SS-N-3 Shaddock range of 315 to 410km (196 to 255 miles), so they could be launched before the vessel came under attack from carrier's aircraft.

The missiles

NATO took note of these Soviet developments but did nothing to copy them until 1967, when the West began developing its own anti-ship missiles. The US Harpoon, the French Exocet, the Italian Otomat and the Norwegian Penguin were the main types that came into service during the 1970s. All of these missiles were similar in concept. The missile launching platform (ship, plane or submarine) would detect the target and pass that information to the missile. The missile would then be launched and keep to a course based on the launch platform's information. In the last part of its flight it would use its own radar to relocate the target and then swoop down to wave level so that the target ship would have difficulty in seeing it. The missile would continue this sea-skimming flight until it hit the target. In the 1982 Falklands War, the loss of the British destroyer HMS *Sheffield* to an Exocet ASM has reinforced the view that the ASMs are the single biggest threat to the surface warship. On the other hand, a warship which carries ASMs is now a far more dangerous ship than in the past.

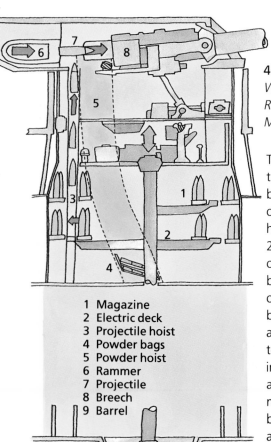

1 Magazine
2 Electric deck
3 Projectile hoist
4 Powder bags
5 Powder hoist
6 Rammer
7 Projectile
8 Breech
9 Barrel

USS New Jersey

406mm 50 Model 1936
Weight: 1730 tonnes (1700 tons)
Rate of Fire: 2 rounds/min/barrel
Maximum Range: 38km (23.5 miles)

The 406mm (16 in) guns mounted in triple turrets in the US Iowa class battleships are both the largest and oldest naval guns in service. The heavy armor-piercing shell (1226kg 2700 lbs) can penetrate 9m (30 ft) of reinforced concrete. The battleships, each of which carry nine of these guns, capable of firing a broadside of 11.17 tonnes (11 tons) at maximum, have been brought back to service after years of being inactive in "mothballs." They are used partly as the platforms for new long-range missiles, and partly for shore bombardment missions. These ships are the best protected war vessels in the world.

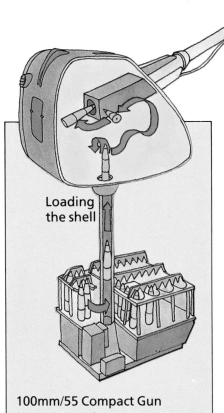

Loading
the shell

100mm/55 Compact Gun
(Creusot-Loire)
Weight: 17.5 tonnes (17 tons)
Maximum Rate of Fire: 90
rounds/minute
Effective Range (surface): 15km
(9 miles); *(air)* 8km (5 miles).

Firing across the bow

Most cruisers, destroyers and frigates
are equipped with two different gun
systems: a medium caliber gun and a
close-in weapon system. The medium
caliber gun, as in the example left, is a
ship's most flexible weapon. It can
engage surface targets, including
those on shore, be used as an anti-
aircraft weapon, help in electronic
warfare by firing shells filled with
chaff and in peacetime to threaten
vessels which refuse to follow the
warship's orders (known as "firing
across the bow").

Close-in weapons systems

The close-in weapon system has been
developed to defend warships against
anti-ship missiles. It is the final layer in
the air defense screen and offers a
high chance of destroying a missile
because of its high rate of fire – 50
rounds per second.

Direction of
radar scan

Turn of
gun

**20mm Vulcan/Phalanx Mk.15
Mod.1 CIWS** (General Dynamics)
Weight: 5.5 tonnes (5.4 tons)
Maximum Rate of Fire: 3000
rounds/minute
Effective Range: 1486m
(4895 ft)

Weapons Systems

A ship's main weapon is made up of a complex and integrated system containing many sub-systems. They can be linked through data bases to other systems within the ship, or through data and video links to systems in other ships, aircraft and shore stations. In consequence, a weapon is now called a weapon system and a collection of systems is termed a suite. Most systems are designed on a modular principle, which allows individual sub-systems to be removed and replaced in a fashion similar to using "LEGO" bricks. This makes maintenance of the system easier and allows the designer to incorporate improvements without having to rebuild the entire system.

Some systems, such as the AEGIS weapons control system, are built as a whole but most are designed to interlock with already existing systems. For example, the US Mark 92 fire control system was designed and developed in Holland from the Signaal WM.20 series of systems. These are used in the warships of many countries (including Holland, West Germany, Italy, Australia and Nigeria) and can control a variety of French, British, Italian and American weapons.

Weapons

On the US Navy's Oliver Hazard Perry class frigate, the Mark 92 controls a variety of defense systems, such as the long-range Standard air defense missile system, the Harpoon anti-ship missile system, the Italian Oto Melara Compact gun, and a Vulcan/Phalanx Mk.15 close-in weapons system. Through information received from the surface (SPS-55) and air (SPS 49) search radars, the Mark 92 uses its own radars to track the target and direct the SPG-60 STIR target illuminating radar to illuminate the target. In turn, each part of the system, like a radar, has its own components, such as an antenna, a transmitter, a receiver, a signal processor and data bases. But the effect of this leaves the physical appearance of a ship, its missiles and antennas largely unchanged for years while in fact substantial internal modifications have been made. Systems usually have a life of 15 years.

AEGIS

This new class of cruiser, the Ticonderoga class, equipped with the AEGIS weapons control system, will form the basis of the US Navy's air defense until well into the next century. Its principal feature is its ability to track and engage multiple air targets. A large number of targets can be tracked at the same time and the system can automatically decide whether to engage or not. It can engage 20 targets at the same time, far more than any other system in the world.

Color coding of the AEGIS system fitted on a Ticonderoga class cruiser.

Yellow – Computer controls for whole AEGIS system

Orange – AEGIS weapons and controls

Red – AEGIS radar panels

Blue – Sonars

CG48 USS Yorktown, Ticonderoga class

American Ticonderoga class AEGIS cruiser
Displacement: 9685 tonnes (9350 tons) full load
Speed: over 30 knots   *Engines:* 4 gas
Turbines: 86,000hp   *Crew:* 346

Defense suites

The systems concept carries over from the design to actual use. Weapon systems are organized into air defense suites, surface warfare suites and anti-submarine warfare suites. Each suite is arranged to provide a layered defense. Taking air defense as an example, a ship will try to confuse an attacking missile or aircraft at the shortest range with its electronic warfare equipment – chaff to blind the radars, decoys to put off heat-seeking missiles and jamming to block radar and radio transmissions. Out to about 1500m (5000 ft) the close-in weapons system will shoot at the target. Out to 8km (5 miles) from the ship, the medium caliber gun 76mm to 152mm (3 in to 6 in) and the point defense surface-to-air missile system will engage the target. Beyond this, the area defense surface-to-air missile system will attempt to hit the target out to ranges of about 55km (34 miles).

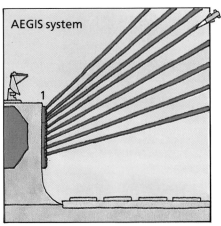

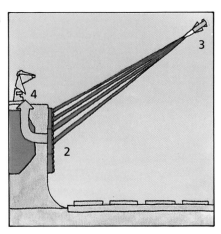

Engaging the target

The AEGIS system uses a very complex radar to detect and track targets. The radar produces wide coverage beams to search for targets (1). If one appears there is a narrow beam to track it (2) while it continues to search for others. When the target (3) comes within engagement range of the Standard missile, the system orders its launch (4) and directs (5) the missile to the general location of the target (6). Finally, the system instructs a third radar (7) to illuminate the target for the missile. At no point is human intervention needed. AEGIS decides which target is most threatening and which has the best chance of being destroyed.

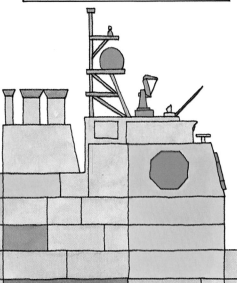

Electronic Defenses

At sea there is nowhere to hide, except beneath it. There are no hills to duck behind and no valleys to conceal oneself in. All attacks from other ships and aircraft must be resisted head-on or else death and injury will follow. Almost any individual attack can be stopped. But the problem lies with saturation attacks, with missiles coming in from every direction and from heights ranging from a few feet above the waves (sea-skimming) up to 14,000m (46,000 ft).

To defeat such mass attacks a ship's defenses must be nimble, reacting quickly to multiple threat through the full range of countermeasures available. That requires that the electronic sensors, fire control system, electronically guided weapons and the electronic countermeasures be fully integrated with each other and with the crew.

Interception and Deception

Despite the complexity and diversity of defensive systems there are, in principle, only two types of action which can be taken: interception or deception. The incoming missiles can either be shot down with missiles and guns or the missile must be deceived on the whereabouts of the target.

Interception depends first on detection. A radar sends out an electronic beam, part of which strikes the missile and returns to the radar as an echo. This echo is analyzed and compared with past echoes in order to measure the range, speed and direction in which the missile is moving plus the angle, called the azimuth, between the ship and the missile. Some radars can also find the height of the missile. With this data, one of the ship's Surface-to-Air Missile (SAM) systems or Close-In Weapons

USSR Kara class cruiser

Systems (CIWS) guns can be fired against the missile. But, if a missile is coming head-on it only exposes a small cross section to the radar beams, thus returning only a small echo.

A small target

For example, the USA's anti-ship missile, the RGM-84A Harpoon, has a diameter of 34cm (14 in) head-on compared to radar cross sections of several feet for an aircraft or a missile sideways. This small size has two important consequences. Firstly, the radar will first see a Harpoon when it is closer than it would have seen a much larger target. Secondly, by flying the missile very close to the sea, it can be hidden in the radar clutter caused by waves. The problem is yet more complex than this, for every advance in detecting a missile, it is paralleled within a few years, by a further technique in hiding the missile. The problems with deception are no less complex.

Chaff dispersal

Defense and decoy

When a ship finds it is being attacked by a missile it will take evasive action. Rockets on the ship are fired to deploy chaff and infrared decoys. Chaff is a mass of thin strips of metal which reflect radar waves, forming a cloud of chaff which looks, to a radar homing missile, like a larger target than the ship itself. The missile is trained to attack the largest target (since these are the most important) and so is seduced away from the ship. The infrared decoys are similar, being heat generating flares to seduce heat-seeking missiles. Meanwhile, the ship itself turns to present its smallest radar and heat reflections by turning its stern or bow to the missile (whichever is quickest).

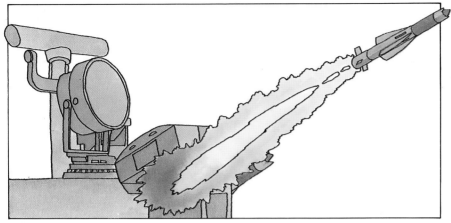

Sea Dart

Semi-active guidance

Semi-active radar guidance is the most common form of guidance for long-range air defense missiles, such as the US Standard and British Sea Dart systems. Once a target is detected it is tracked until it is in missile range. Then an "illuminating" radar shines a radar beam at the target. The missile is launched, and with a radar receiver in its nose, it homes in on the greatest radar returns reflected by the target.

Jamming

Missiles like Harpoon or the French Exocet normally have their own small radar in the nose of the missile. The electronic beam that they send out can be picked up by listening devices on the ship known as Electronic Support Measures (ESM). The data gathered by the ESM can then be passed on to the radars, making their job of detection easier by knowing what to look for, or deception measures can be taken. This can be to try and decoy the missile, or to use Electronic Counter Measures (ECM) to try and blind the radar of the attacking

missile. This is called jamming. There are two main ways of jamming; barrage jamming and spot jamming.

In barrage jamming the whole spectrum of radar frequencies is blasted with random radio noise in the hope of confusing the attacking radar. It cannot tell the difference between the echoes from the target and the noise. Spot jamming is the same except it jams on a particular frequency of the attacking radar. Both forms of jamming have their disadvantages and can be defeated.

Seawolf

Command guidance

Command guidance is commonly used on shorter range air defense missiles like Seawolf because it allows a quicker response. One radar tracks the target, and a second tracks the missile. A computer determines how to bring the two together, a third dish transmitting the course changes to the missile. At long range the beams of a radar fan out, making them less accurate, which is why this system is restricted to short range engagements.

Infrared decoys

Ship turning as missile is deflected

Carrier

The carrier is the principal warship in the world's most powerful navies. France, USSR, Italy, Spain and Britain operate a few modern, small carriers. India, Argentina, Brazil and Australia each have a single small old carrier. Only the United States can afford to operate a fleet of 13 large supercarriers. The Soviet Union, which currently has five small carriers, is building its first large one which should be ready for operations by about 1990. But, at the same time, the US is building three larger carriers with the aim of having 15 available for operations at any one time by the early 1990s. The US's most recently commissioned carrier, the USS *Carl Vinson* of the Nimitz class, displaces over 95,520 tonnes (94,000 tons) and carries over 90 aircraft and helicopters. In comparison, the largest of the "small" carriers, the USSR's *Kharkov* of the Kiev class, is half the size – 42,700 tonnes (42,000 tons), carrying about 33 aircraft and helicopters.

USS America

The flight deck of the USS *Carl Vinson* is 327m (1072 ft) long and 77m (252 ft) wide. The angled flight deck, which juts out to port, is 237m (780 ft) long. The angled flight deck is used for landing operations, although it does have two catapults for launching aircraft. Most launches, however, occur from the two bow catapults. This allows the *Carl Vinson* to launch four aircraft at a time, or to launch two aircraft while recovering aircraft launched earlier. While on the carrier, the aircraft are parked on the flight deck or are taken down to the 8m (26 ft) high hangar by one of four lifts mounted on the side of the ship. The hangar can house between 35 to 40 percent of the carrier's aircraft and is used for maintenance and repair.

This work ranges from routine checks on aircraft electrical systems, to major jobs such as changing the aircraft's engines. The difference between the large US carriers and all the other small ones (except those of the French Navy) is not just a matter of size.

V/STOL aircraft

The US and French carriers have catapults to help launch aircraft which would otherwise need about 2 to 3000m (6 to 9000 ft) of runway to take off. The other carriers do not have catapults (or arrester wires) because they use aircraft which can take off and land vertically. Aside from helicopters there are two aircraft which can fly in this way, the British-developed Harrier and the Soviet Yak-36 Forger. These aircraft do not have the same high performance because so much of their energy is used in vertical operations. They can carry fewer weapons a shorter distance. They can, however, fly from much smaller, cheaper ships. This allows fleets which cannot afford a larger carrier to still give air cover to its ships. Providing fighter cover for your own ships and bombers while attacking the enemy is the role of a carrier, so they are themselves, a prime target. Many consider the carrier the queen of the seas and, like any queen, the carrier is always well guarded.

The flight deck of an aircraft carrier

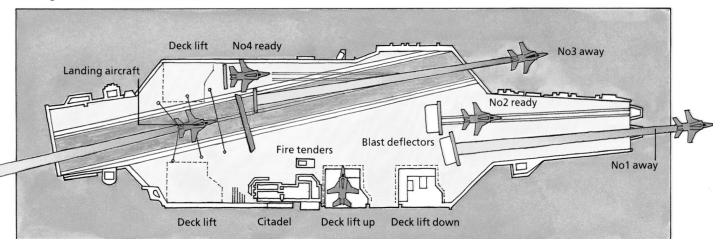

Catapults

The catapult is driven by steam powered pistons. The steam is fed from the engines to a pressure valve. This regulates the action of the trolley.

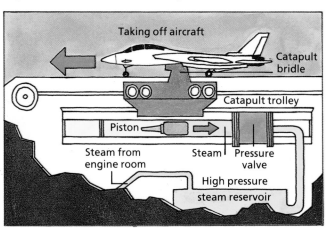

Arrester wires

The wire is attached to a piston in a braking cylinder. The movement of the piston forces out the braking fluid. This causes the braking motion.

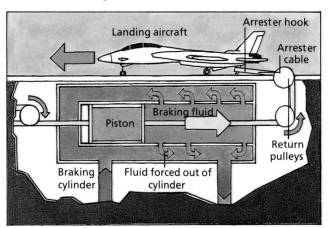

The Carrier Battle Group

Carriers never sail alone. They are always surrounded by a number of cruisers, destroyers and frigates whose task is to protect the carrier; this is the carrier battle group (CVBG). This is an American organization since no other nations operate large carriers, although countries with small carriers operate similar formations. The group is normally formed up into one or two rough circles around the carrier. The inner circle is made up of ships responsible for the air defense of the carrier. The outer circle is more concerned with defending the carrier from submarine attacks; and beyond the escorting ships, the carrier's aircraft form a shield over the whole formation.

Cruisers and destroyers

Cruisers are the largest general-purpose ships, meaning that they are good at everything, although the Soviets and Italians tend to specialize their cruisers for either hunting submarines or (the USSR only) attacking carriers. In the US, there was an attempt to make all cruisers nuclear-powered. This would have enabled them to go unrefueled,

USS Dwight D. Eisenhower

and so reduce the number of supply ships following in the wake of the CVBG. The penalty was very expensive ships and the idea was abandoned after nine had been built. These include the USS *Long Beach*, the world's first nuclear-powered surface ship and the first warship to be armed with guided missiles as the main weapon.

The carrier battle group

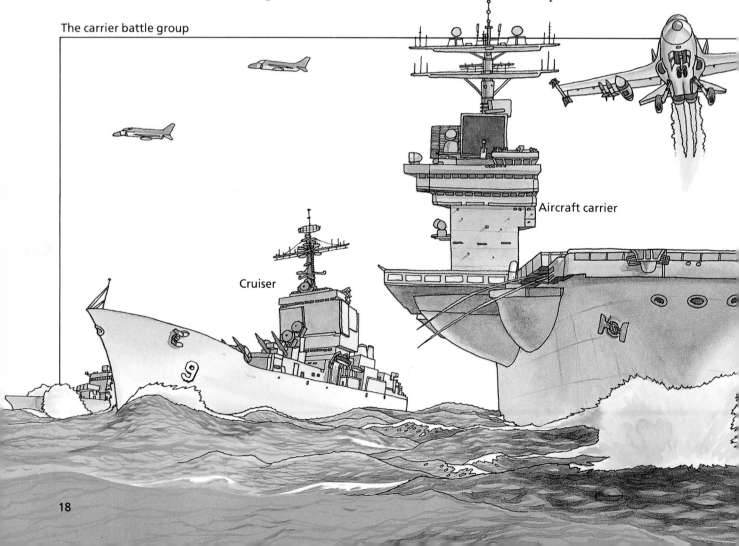

Cruiser

Aircraft carrier

Destroyers are smaller than cruisers, normally displacing between 4070 tonnes (4000 tons) and 8130 tonnes (8000 tons). In the US Navy there are two types, "DDG" (anti-air) destroyers, such as the 23 Charles F. Adams class, or the soon-to-be-built Burke class, which will have a major air defense system such as the AEGIS system, or the similar air defense system, Tartar.

"DD" destroyers, such as the 31 DD-963 Spruance class, specialize in anti-submarine operations. Both DDGs and DDs would be present in the carrier battle group, providing the back-up for the cruisers and the outer anti-submarine screen.

Frigates and corvettes

A frigate displaces between 1525 tonnes (1500 tons) and 4070 tonnes (4000 tons) and is standardized as being a vessel which is very good at a particular mission, normally anti-submarine, and which is able to operate on the high seas. Ships under about 1525 tonnes (1500 tons) are not large enough to sail well in heavy seas and do not have enough endurance to sail far beyond the

USS Constellation

coast. These vessels of a smaller displacement are called corvettes. The frigate is not designed as a carrier escort. Its real role is to escort the less important ships, in other words, those ships that are not fighting warships. These include amphibious assault ships, supply ships and merchant ships.

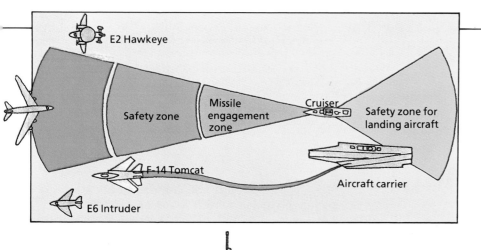

Safety zones

When protecting the carrier it is important not to confuse friendly aircraft and submarines with enemy ones. Aircraft from the carrier, therefore, must fly through "safe" corridors when landing or taking off. The aircraft must then fly out to over 160km (100 miles) from the carrier group. Between about 95km (60 miles) and 48km (30 miles) is a "Safety Zone" where neither aircraft nor ship's missiles must fire. Aircraft chasing an enemy plane into the safety zone must give up, allowing the enemy to fly on to the group where, at under 48km (30 miles) the ship's missiles will attack it.

Life on Board

Life on an aircraft carrier, the largest of warships, is often compared to living in a small town made up only of men. Even the US's smallest carrier, the 68,000 tonne (67,000 ton) USS *Midway* has a crew of 4600, working the ship 24 hours a day for often over 100 days without touching land. The crew frequently works 12-hour shifts, and longer if there are flying operations going on. This high pitch of work, over such a long period without rest, demands a high level of support for the normal activities of life: 130 cooks and 200 mess hands provide and clear away four meals a day. There are three dentists, and a 22-bed hospital with operating and X ray rooms, and a laundry which can clean three tons of clothes and linen a day.

It is from the Combat Information Center that the entire ship and her aircraft are controlled.

Jogging is one form of exercise for the crew. Six times around the flight deck of an aircraft carrier equals approximately 4.8km (3 miles).

Relaxation on board

A printing office which produces 1200 copies of the ship's daily newspaper as well as handling the carrier's normal paperwork. A two-channel television station supplies some 2000 TV sets with "home-made" programs and programs relayed by satellite to a nearby shore station and flown out to the carrier. Exercise is provided by using the flight deck and hangar when there is no flying, with jogging, basketball, volleyball, wrestling and boxing. An empty room next to the funnel which is normally at 45°C (140°F) is used as a sauna. The crews of US carriers are also the largest consumer of *used* golf balls in the world. They buy them in bulk during shore leave so that they can practise their golf strokes while on sea duties, on the flight deck. Most of the balls, of course, go over the side

of the deck, which is why they do not buy new ones.

Despite all this, life on the carrier can be dull and isolated. Its size makes it easy to get lost in, with 19 deck levels (all connected by ladders – only the aircraft use lifts) and a surface area, at the flight deck, of 1.6 hectares (4 acres).

Each passageway junction has a map posted by it. Some of the crew, particularly in the engine room, rarely get to see daylight. The most important days for the crew are when the mail comes and when they are allowed to go ashore during a port visit.

Work on board

The reason for the carrier, however, is to get aircraft aloft. The flight deck during flight operations is a confusing and dangerous place. The noise of aircraft, whose engines can produce 18.8 tonnes (18.5 tons) of thrust, means everyone on the flight deck must wear large ear protectors. This means they cannot hear what is going on and must use their eyes and be constantly alert.

Because of the danger, the flight deck crew is highly trained and wears bright-colored jerseys, green for the catapult crew, red for the weapons handlers, purple for the refuelers, blue for the aircraft handlers and yellow for the supervisors. They operate in small teams working to a flexible system which allows them to recover and launch the 65 aircraft that the *Midway* carries.

The *Midway*, like all US carriers, also carries a stockpile of nuclear weapons. These are secured under elaborate fail-safe precautions and guarded, 24 hours a day, by armed Marines.

The crew relaxing on the carrier.

Crew comparison

	Name	Country	Ship's personnel	Air personnel
Large aircraft carrier	Nimitz	USA	203 officers 3205 men	366 officers 2512 men
Small aircraft carrier	Invincible	Britain	131 officers 869 men	318 (*total*)
Battleship	Iowa	USA	74 officers 1579 men	
Cruiser	Slava	Russia	30 officers 490 men	
Destroyer	Georges Leygues	France	105 officers 111 men	
Frigate	Oliver Hazard Perry	USA	32 officers 183 men	
Corvette	Pietro de Cristofaro	Italy	8 officers 123 men	
Minesweeper	Tripartite	Belgium, France Netherlands	6 officers 42 men	
Fast Attack Craft	Osa	Russia	15 (*total*)	

Aircraft are very fast and the flight deck comparatively small. It is therefore a skilled job to guide an aircraft on to the carrier's deck.

On a large aircraft carrier, the kitchens are staffed by 130 cooks who have to prepare meals for the 6 000 crew that operate the vessel.

Aviation gas is highly flammable, and special, highly trained crew members are constantly alert on the flight deck for any accidents that may occur.

Four meals a day, the fourth at midnight, are cooked for the crew teams who run the ship 24 hours every day while the ship is at sea.

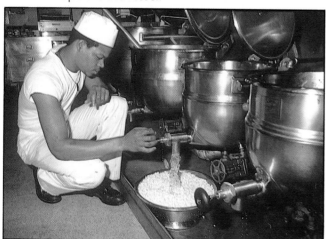

Fleet Catalogue

Although the aircraft carriers, battleships and nuclear-powered cruisers tend to receive most of the public attention because of their size and immense power, all fleets are made up of a balanced force of many smaller types of warships. These vessels are normally of three general types, escort vessels, coastal vessels and specialized vessels. Below is a selection of these vessels, including three escort ships. The largest is the destroyer USS *Farragut* of the Coontz class, and slightly smaller is a frigate of the Niteroi class of the Brazilian Navy. The smallest is the corvette of the Erin'mi class of the Nigerian Navy, designed and built in Britain.

Niteroi class frigate

The escorts

The three ships represent the full range of escort ships. The 4800-tonne (4700-ton) *Farragut* is designed to escort US carriers across the world's oceans. She has a moderate suite of anti-submarine and surface warfare weapons to help protect the carrier from surface ship and submarine attack. Her primary weapon, though, is her air defense missile system. This has a magazine of 40 Standard missiles, of the long-range version, fired from a twin arm missile launcher on the destroyer's quarterdeck. Above the launcher are the system's two fire control radars. The system occupies most of the aft end of the ship.

In comparison, the Niteroi class frigate is a much more general purpose, but weaker, vessel. Brazil has six Niterois, four of which are designed for particularly hunting submarines.

USS Farragut destroyer

Submarine hunters and patrol craft

The submarine hunters have a small air defense missile system and a medium caliber gun (76-152mm (3-6 in)) but have three anti-submarine weapons. A helicopter, which has a missile that drops a torpedo at the end of its flight; torpedo tubes, where a rocket launcher drops a bomb which explodes at a preset depth (a depth charge), and a rack containing depth charges which can be rolled off the stern of the ship into the sea. They are, at 3250 tonnes (3200 tons), smaller than the USS *Farragut* and are designed to escort any other vessels on the high seas.

The Erin'mi class is much smaller at 864 tonnes (850 tons), fully loaded. Its size does not allow it to carry any major weapons, such as the Standard missile system or a helicopter. Instead it has a 76mm (3 in) gun, a depth charge-throwing rocket launcher and a small air defense missile system. This is a weak but balanced armament which allows the corvette to carry out the corvette's main mission, that of escort and patrol in inshore, local sea areas.

Specialised vessels

Destroyer, frigate and corvette escort vessels are always thought of as warships since they can carry out several missions with normal weapons. However, several warships carry out specialized missions for which they need either few or no weapons. This includes minehunters, such as HMS *Bronington*, below, and amphibious assault ships like HMS *Sir Percivale*, below. As with the escorts, mine countermeasures vessels (which include minehunters) and amphibious assault vessels come in a range of sizes, depending on how far out to sea they are intended to go.

Lastly, coastal patrol work is carried out in several navies by the fast patrol craft, armed with, normally, a 76mm (3 in) gun and anti-ship missiles as with the 52M vessel below. Vessels like these are particularly usefully deployed in narrow passages of water, such as rivers, where the movement of larger vessels is restricted, and can be used as a back-up to small, lightly armed patrol boats which are used to enforce the laws of the sea on navigation, fishing, smuggling and piracy.

Erin'mi class corvette

52M Fast Attack Craft

HMS Bronington minesweeper

HMS Sir Percivale

Anti-Submarine Warfare

Anti-Submarine Warfare (ASW) is the most difficult form of combat undertaken by the surface ships of the fleet. The world's four largest ocean-going fleets, the US, the Soviet, the French and the British, all see ASW as their most important role.

Friendly submarines mount standing patrols to intercept attacking submarines. Aircraft are directed by ships to "pounce" on submarines which "leak" through the barriers, while the surface ships mount round-the-clock protective screens around carriers and convoys. The best method of submarine detection is to listen for the sound it makes but if the submarine does not want to be detected, it will move slowly and carefully, making as little noise as possible in an attempt to creep up on its target.

This means that the noises to be detected are very faint and can get drowned out by the noise of the sea itself and sea animals, as well as the noises that the ship makes with its own engines. Thus, to hear a submarine, the ship itself must be quiet.

Underwater listening

The listening device is called sonar, and can work in two ways. Either it just listens (passive sonar) or it sends out a noise and listens for the echo bounced back off the submarine's hull (active sonar). A ship will often carry three different sonar systems.

These are a sonar mounted at the bow or under the hull which can work actively or passively, a towed array sonar on a long cable (to remove it as far as possible from the ship's noises), and a helicopter equipped with either a dipping sonar or sonobuoys.

The dipping sonar is a smaller version of the bow sonar and is dipped into the water at the end of a long cable while the helicopter hovers. The sonobuoy is a small, "throwaway" passive sonar, which is dropped into the water to transmit the information it gathers. The towed array sonar is used to detect the target first. The helicopter or mine-hunter is used to pinpoint the target and attack it.

Hunting the submarine

Hunting submarines is so difficult that almost all warships have some ASW capability. Each warship has the ability to detect and destroy a submarine, and the more ASW ships available, the higher the chance of one of them being in the right place to attack. In this way it is hoped that an attacking submarine force would be gradually worn down. This is called a battle of attrition. Likewise the submarines are involved in a battle of attrition, trying to sink a number of ships before they have to return to base or are sunk themselves.

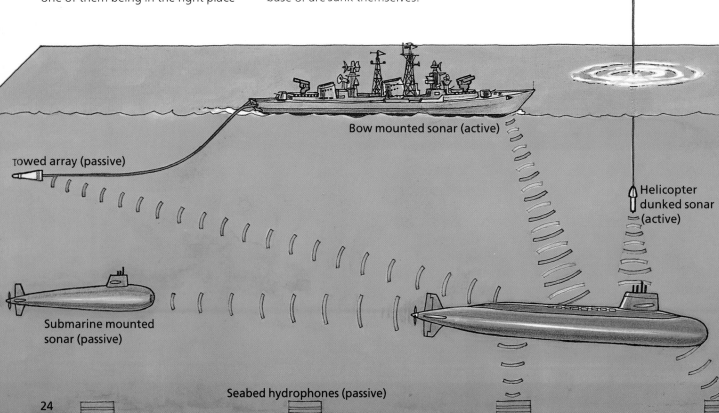

Towed array (passive)

Bow mounted sonar (active)

Helicopter dunked sonar (active)

Submarine mounted sonar (passive)

Seabed hydrophones (passive)

Sea King with Stringray missile

Anti-submarine missile Ikara

This is a complex arrangement but the sea is very large and, in comparison, a submarine is very small. Ships very rarely hunt for submarines alone. Instead, they cooperate with other ships, helicopters, patrol aircraft and friendly submarines, gaining information from all these, and from a series of fixed passive sonars mounted on the seabed in channels, where it is believed an enemy submarine will pass. The information gathered is mostly processed ashore at the fleet headquarters.

Control and attack

It is from there that the ASW battle is controlled and fought across an ocean. This ensures the greatest chance of finding and tracking a submarine.

Locating the submarine is the most difficult problem but attacking and destroying it is hardly any easier. The main weapon is the torpedo, fired by the ship or dropped by the missile, helicopter or aircraft. The torpedo has a small active/passive sonar to guide it on to the target.

Destroying the submarine

The standard ASW weapon is the lightweight torpedo. It travels at 40 knots for 11,000m (36,000 ft) to a depth of at least 300m (980 ft).

Until it detects a target, the torpedo will go through a preset search pattern in order to thoroughly cover the area in which the submarine is expected to be.

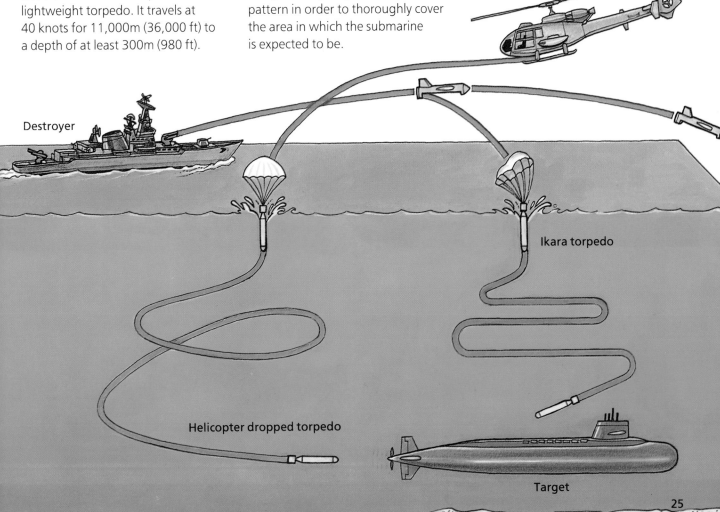

Destroyer

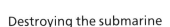
Helicopter dropped torpedo

Ikara torpedo

Target

The Amphibious Squadron

Many navies maintain a Marine force under their control. Marines are soldiers specially trained in the techniques of landing on a hostile shore. Most marine forces number a few thousand and are capable of capturing a medium-sized target such as an island or a port. The US Marine Corps, however, is quite different. With 194,000 men and women, it is about ten times larger than any other Marine force and with its own air force of over 500 combat aircraft and helicopters it is capable of capturing large territories. The Marines can loiter off the coast in international waters for several months before needing to be relieved and can either threaten or assist a country depending on the circumstances. Marines are also frequently used in peacekeeping forces.

The need to land the Marines on to an exposed, and often hostile, beach demands a special series of ships ranging from landing craft of a few tons – to actually land the Marines on the beach – to ships the size of aircraft carriers – to bring them.

The vehicles

At the small end of the scale are the landing craft which come in a variety of sizes from Landing Vehicle Tracked Personnel, an amphibious troop carrier, to Landing Craft (LC) of increasing size. These include LC Vehicle & Personnel; LC Utility; LC Mechanized and the new LC Air Cushion, a hovercraft designed to get the Marines onto the beaches quickly. The landing craft are transported by a series of landing ships. The Landing Ship Tank provides heavy support to the landing craft and can unload heavy equipment directly on to the beach.

The larger Landing Platform Dock has a dock well in the stern in which it carries its own landing craft and a flight deck. The even larger Landing Platform Helicopter has a flight deck and hangar for about 20 helicopters. Largest of all is the Landing Helicopter Assault which has both a dock well and a flight deck and hangar. Civilian ferries can also be converted into Ro-Ro (Roll on-Roll off) craft for military use, to transport heavy equipment.

USS Tarawa class

The Landing Helicopter Assault ships of the USS Tarawa class at 40,000 tonnes (39,400 tons), full load, are the size of an aircraft carrier. They carry over 20 helicopters and aircraft (vertical take off and landing, Harrier type). The dock can handle four 380-tonne (375-ton) landing craft, and the ship carries another six 61 tonne (60 ton) craft. It can carry over 1000 marines, plus their commanding staff, for which it is equipped with extensive communications (including satellite links). It is fitted with a 300-bed hospital complete with operating rooms, X ray room, laboratories and intensive care facilities.

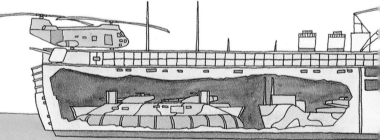

Helicopter landing to embark Marines

Tank landing vessel, USS Saginaw

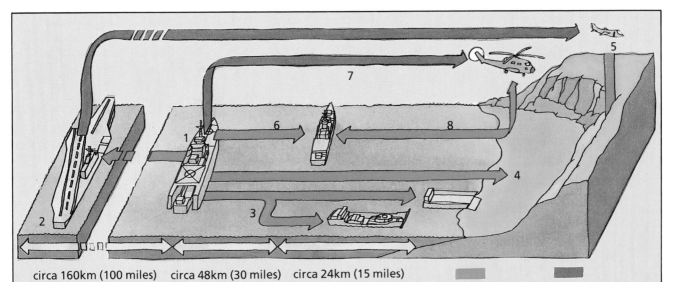

circa 160km (100 miles)   circa 48km (30 miles)   circa 24km (15 miles)

Communications   Command

Amphibious Squadron: Command and Control

The Landing Helicopter Assault (LHA) ship coordinates all the assault forces as well as the air and surface cover provided by a Carrier Battle Group (1). The Carrier provides air strikes, fighter cover and reconnaissance for the beach landing (2). The LHA controls the unloading of troops and equipment (3), onto the beach (4). The battalion headquarters on the beach organizes the marines and asks for fire support help with the landing (5). The LHA instructs the escorting warships about fire support (6). The LHA controls air activity over the beach (7). Troops ashore and helicopters control the fire of the warships (8).

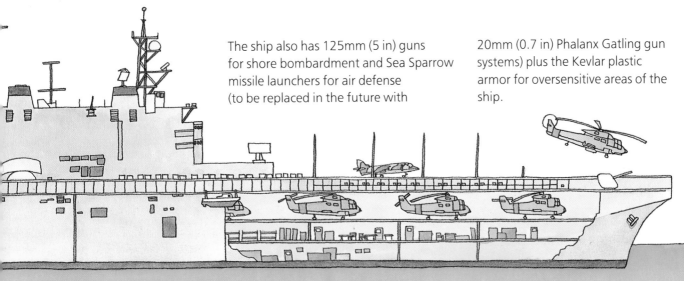

The ship also has 125mm (5 in) guns for shore bombardment and Sea Sparrow missile launchers for air defense (to be replaced in the future with 20mm (0.7 in) Phalanx Gatling gun systems) plus the Kevlar plastic armor for oversensitive areas of the ship.

Civilian ferry converted to Ro-Ro vessel

Hovercraft landing vehicle

Supply, Support and Reactivation

All navies are supported by a network of ports and bases. At these places warships can be repaired, cleaned, refueled and rearmed. The ship's crew can rejoin their families and rest. In addition, on shore are the naval headquarters, air bases for naval aircraft, and colleges where sailors learn to operate and maintain the complex equipment. There are also warehouses where stocks of all naval items, from missiles to uniforms, are kept. The navies of the US, the USSR, France and Britain, however, often operate their ships far away from the homeland and without having nearby, friendly bases and so they take their own backup with them in a fleet of special ships.

The US Navy, which hopes to have a fleet of 600 warships (including submarines) by about 1990, has the largest fleet of support ships and vessels. This fleet is so large that there are twice as many support vessels as there are combat ships. These support vessels can be divided into four groups.

There are those ships that maintain the warships in distant waters by resupplying them while they are in the open seas. Other ships set up temporary naval bases on the coast where no port facilities exist. Thirdly, there are ships which sail between the US and the country's more remote bases, keeping them well supplied. Finally, there are the vessels which operate within the naval bases.

HMAS Supply ship

The groups

The first group is organized into Underway Replenishment Groups (URG). These sail between the bases and the carrier battle groups, refueling, rearming and resupplying the warships with food, medicine, mail and so on. This allows the warships to stay in the combat zone for longer periods. The supply ships carry a variety of cargo-handling equipment, to pass liquids (like oil) and solids (such as food) to the warship as the two ships sail side by side.

Refueling at sea

USS New Jersey in dry dock for reactivation refit

Repair and reactivation

Ships become old. After 25 to 30 years of constant pounding by the seas, the hull and machinery is normally considered too worn to be worth further repair and the ship is scrapped. Some of the large ships, however, are expensive to replace and it is cheaper to dismantle and rebuild them, replacing the worn parts. Thus, the US Navy is putting its carriers through a Service Life Extension Program which involves a two-year rebuild in order to give each a further 15 years of life. The US Navy also has four battleships which were not needed and so were mothballed. These are now being reactivated, re-quipping them with modern weapons.

The ships used to set up temporary naval bases, or supplement existing ones if they become overcrowded, include repair ships with special workshops and heavy lifting gear. These can repair most breakdowns and can patch up battle damage so that the damaged warship can limp to a main naval base for major repairs. Others include hospital ships for treating wounded soldiers and sailors, and tenders. These act like "mother ships" to small or cramped warships such as patrol ships, frigates and submarines.

The third group of support ships mainly includes ordinary merchant ships, such as tankers and freighters, for taking supplies between the US's 25 naval bases. Finally, there is the largest group, of harbor vessels. These are the tugs, barges and floating docks. The floating dock can be moved, by tugs, to different bases, when it is too expensive to give each base a large dock, for carrying out major repairs. Many of the vessels described above are crewed by civilians rather than by naval personnel and they provide indispensable support to a navy.

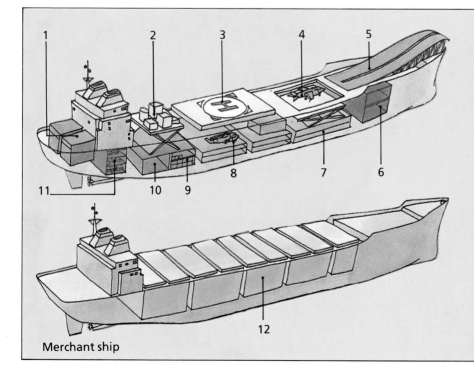

Civilian merchant ships are often needed for military purposes. Skilled engineers can convert an ordinary container ship into a small fighting vessel, with aircraft capability, in a short time.

1 Stores containers
2 Stores on scissor lift
3 Helicopter landing pad
4 Harrier aircraft
5 Harrier ski-jump
6 Workshops
7 Power generators
8 Aircraft hangar
9 Magazines
10 Stores
11 Living quarters
12 Ordinary containers

Merchant ship

Coastal Defense

There are three main elements in coastal defense. There is the Mine Counter Measures (MCM) force of minesweepers and minehunters which try to keep the ports, harbors and shipping lanes free of obstruction by minefields. Then, there are the patrol boats, armed with guns or missiles, responsible for checking the coastal shipping and protecting the offshore assets such as oil rigs or fishing grounds. They also have responsibility for fighting in narrow channels where larger warships do not have enough room to maneuver. Finally, there are the maritime patrol aircraft which maintain a constant surveillance over the coastal waters. In wartime, these aircraft track and attack enemy ships and submarines but their main peacetime role is to act as the ocean's policemen.

Coastal defense vessels

Coastal defense vessels tend to be small, with normally a displacement of less than 1020 tonnes (1000 tons) and a crew of less than 50. This is because they do not need great range, and are not expected to stay out in stormy seas for long periods. This makes them comparatively cheap to build, and many small navies are equipped only with coastal defense boats. The largest coastal defense forces, however, are operated by China and the USSR, who have over 1000 and over 800 MCM vessels and patrol boats, respectively, in their navies, and more operated by their border security organizations. This ensures that it is very difficult to get into or out of these countries despite the fact that they both have very long coastlines.

Mine detonation

There are four different types of sea mines. These are magnetic, acoustic, pressure and contact. Magnetic mines are set off by the magnetism of the ship's metal hull. Acoustic mines detonate on hearing the noise of the ship's engine. Pressure mines detonate because of the change in pressure caused by the ship's bow wave passing over it. Contact mines explode if they hit a ship.

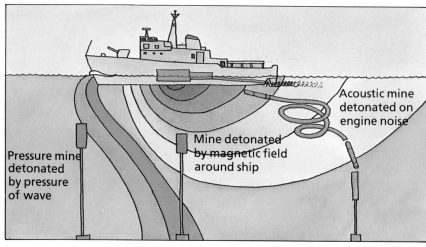

Acoustic mine detonated on engine noise

Mine detonated by magnetic field around ship

Pressure mine detonated by pressure of wave

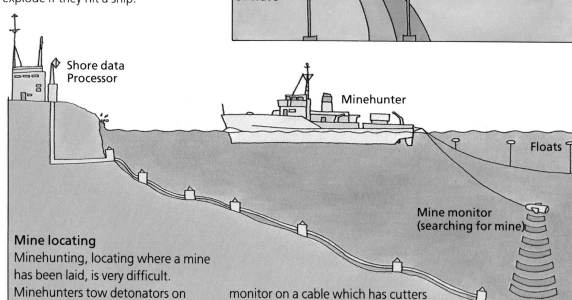

Shore data Processor

Minehunter

Floats

Detonator

Mine monitor (searching for mine)

Mine locating

Minehunting, locating where a mine has been laid, is very difficult. Minehunters tow detonators on floating cables to monitor the seabed, and explode any mines they find. Another method used by the minehunting ship is to tow a depth monitor on a cable which has cutters along its length.

These cut the moored mines, allowing them to float upwards. As they reach the surface, they can be exploded by gun fire from the ship.

Sonars, mounted on the ship, can form a picture of the seabed.

Russian Fast Attack Craft

Patrol vessels

Patrol boats tend to come in two forms, small, slow, lightly armed craft used mainly in peacetime and more powerful, Fast Attack Craft (FAC). FACs are either armed with anti-ship missiles, torpedoes or guns. They normally have a displacement of about 255 tonnes (250 tons) and are capable of speeds of over 40 knots, the fastest being the Soviet Sarancha class which, at 325 tonnes (320 tons), is said to be capable of 58 knots. Missile armed FACs are the most common, though many of these are now being equipped with guns to protect themselves from air attack.

MCM vessels

MCM vessels are very specialized; they hunt and destroy mines. Many have hulls made of wood or glass reinforced plastic to give them a lower magnetic field than a metal ship, so that they can deal with magnetically detonated mines. Most have towing gear for cables to cut the mine from its moorings or sound generating equipment to detonate acoustic mines. Others operate remote controlled, unmanned submarines or boats which enter the danger area. Helicopters can also be used to tow rafts through the water, which simulate a passing ship, to detonate the mine.

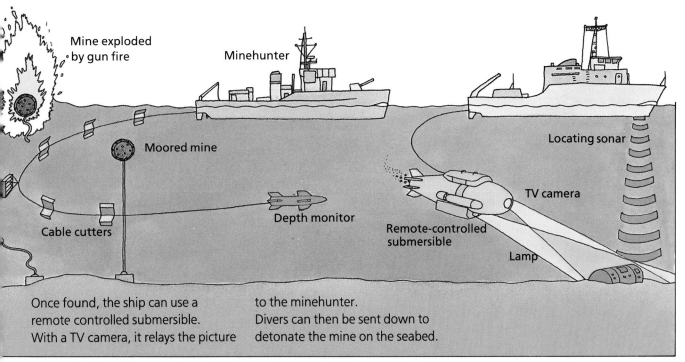

Mine exploded by gun fire

Minehunter

Moored mine

Locating sonar

Cable cutters

Depth monitor

TV camera

Remote-controlled submersible

Lamp

Once found, the ship can use a remote controlled submersible. With a TV camera, it relays the picture to the minehunter. Divers can then be sent down to detonate the mine on the seabed.

The Future

There are currently many ideas which may gain widespread application in the future. These include ideas on new hull forms, new methods of missile guidance, new V/STOL aircraft designs, new guided shells fired from guns, and new computer equipment.

Hull forms

The classic hull form used for most warships is for a long, slim ship, normally about ten times longer than its width. This has certain advantages, such as higher speeds but, at a cost, to the amount of equipment that it can carry. To make the ship go faster, hydrofoils can be used.

Making ships carry more equipment is another area of interest. This can be done by making warship hull forms stubbier, as the US Navy is doing with some of its future destroyers, or by using hulls which go deeper into water than normal hulls or by using twin hulls.

Defense systems

Another area for making warship improvements is in the guidance systems for missiles and guns. It is hoped that very long-range missiles can be made more accurate by using information from navigation satellites to tell the missile exactly where it is. Another important thing is to make systems which shoot down a lot of targets at the same time. Thus, various ideas are in development as to how air defense missiles can either share or operate on reduced guidance information, so that more missiles can intercept a large number of multiple targets at the same time.

Finally, computers with artificial intelligence are expected to enter service in the 1990s, with very important changes apart from simple decision-making. Firstly, they will be able to understand human speech, and secondly it will be able to both see, using cameras and understand, to some extent, what it sees.

USS Vincennes under construction

Surface Warships
History and Development

The warships of the 20th century can easily be divided into two distinct eras. The first was the era of the battleship, which started at the beginning of the century and continued through to the beginning of the Second World War. As the role of the battleship waned, so the aircraft carrier came to the fore as it took over in importance in general naval warfare in 1940 and continues to the present day. Each has dominated its respective era, being the most important warships afloat, a navy's approximate strength could be measured by the number of these vessels that the navy possessed.

The gun

The battleship era was dominated by the gun; it was the most important naval weapon. Battleships were the only warships that were large enough to carry the big, heavy guns, and as a consequence they were the most powerful ships.

Smaller ships, such as cruisers, frigates and destroyers, were also assessed by the caliber of the guns that they carried on board. Heavy cruiser classes were equipped with 203mm (8 inch) guns and the Light cruiser class was usually fitted with 152mm (6 inch) guns. Destroyers had smaller caliber guns, varying from 127mm to 105mm (5 to 4 inch) guns, and frigates carried only the lower range, 105mm (4 inch) gun, as they were designed primarily as escort vessels and they were, and still are, smaller than cruisers and destroyers.

The aircraft

Although the aircraft carrier had already been invented during the First World War, the designs were very primitive and not very effective. The *Furious* is a good example. She was initially designed as a cruiser, but underwent many later refits to accommodate aircraft. This was because it was realized that ships could be used to carry the aircraft, and, therefore, extend the range of air warfare away from the land. But the aircraft carrier was not recognized as being the primary warship until the Second World War.

The Second World War

In the Second World War, most of the battleships were relegated to the role of protecting the aircraft carriers. The battleships usually carried large numbers of anti-aircraft guns which helped to protect the vulnerable carrier from air attack. It was not until after the Second World War that developments in naval technology led to the invention of the missile.

Missiles

Missiles have a far longer range than guns and they are more accurate. This is because the missile could be guided to the target while it was already in flight. Missiles, however, did not have the range of an aircraft, or, more importantly, the accuracy at longer ranges. So the carrier remained the most important warship.

Today, with the advancements in modern technology, missiles are becoming much more accurate at these longer ranges, diminishing the carrier's dominant role as the missiles can be carried by other warships. Distributing the fire power among many ships reduces the vulnerability of any single vessel. The US have 14 aircraft carriers and these would have been the prime target on any attack on the fleet. But fitting long range missiles, such as Tomahawk, to the cruisers, destroyers and frigates means that instead of only 14 ships which can attack targets hundreds of miles away, there will be soon be several hundred. This has also freed the cruisers, destroyers and frigates from the role of only escorting the carriers. With their own long range missiles, they can carry out tasks independent of the carriers.

This has led to the reactivation of the old Iowa class battleships, which had been mothballed. Now they are undergoing refitting with long range missiles. The Soviet Union are building their own large cruisers, the Kirov class, which will have large missile batteries. Both of these ships will form the center of non-aircraft carrier task groups.

Mikasa (1902, Japan)

Built in Britain for the Imperial Japanese Navy, this battleship served as the flagship of Admiral Togo during the Russo-Japanese War 1904-1905. This was the first modern naval war of this century. In it, Japan destroyed the naval power of Imperial Russia. Firstly, she crippled Russia's naval forces in the Pacific by a surprise attack with torpedo boats at the very beginning of the war while the Russians were still in port. Then she destroyed the Russian fleet sent from Europe around the world to relieve their Pacific Squadron. Despite the fact that gun-armed ships were about to undergo a revolution in design, this was the last naval battle between such vessels. The Mikasa was armed with four 305mm (12 in) and fourteen 152mm (6 in) guns, and she now stands as a memorial.

Dreadnought (1906, Britain)

This battleship marked a turning point in capital ship design, marking the beginning of the last phase of gun-only armed ships. Unlike the *Mikasa*, the *Dreadnought* carried ten 305mm (12 in) guns. She was also faster than any previous battleship and built in the shortest time for any capital ship this century – 366 days. By the outset of the First World War in 1914, refinements to the *Dreadnought*'s basic design principle had already made her class, which was called after her, obsolete and she was soon withdrawn from the main fleet to secondary duties. The only action she saw was in ramming and sinking a submarine, the U-29, in 1915.

Scharnhorst (1907, Germany)

When completed, this cruiser, with her sister *Gneisenau*, was already outdated in design by the *Dreadnought* and her cousin, *Invincible*. Nonetheless, *Scharnhorst*, flagship of the German Far East Squadron under Vice Admiral Graf von Spee, led a small group of German ships in the Battle of Coronel (off Chile), where a

Dreadnought

Scharnhorst

British squadron was defeated. Britain was shocked at its first naval defeat for over 100 years and sent a powerful force under *Invincible* to destroy the Germans. Both *Scharnhorst* and her sister were caught and sunk at the Battle of Falklands in the South Atlantic in 1914.

Invincible (1908, Britain)

After the success of *Dreadnought* it was decided to do the same for cruisers. Since the *Dreadnought* was as fast as many cruisers, the latter had to be made faster and since *Dreadnought* could outgun all cruisers, they had to be given guns of

a similar size if they were not to be overwhelmed before escaping – for the job of a cruiser in 1908 was reconnaissance. The result was the fast, all big gun battlecruiser, the *Invincible*. *Invincible* and her sisters dominated other cruisers, though the Germans soon built their own battlecruisers. Britain lied about the design of *Invincible*, letting it be known to the Germans that she would be much weaker than she was in reality, tricking the Germans into making their ships weaker. She could not, however, stand and fight against battleships. To obtain extra speed the battlecruisers were very light on armor protection.

Emden

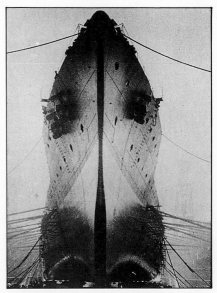
Kongo

Emden *(1909, Germany)*
The creation of the battlecruiser meant that cruisers became very expensive. Yet, to cover the vast European empires of the time, many cruisers were needed. The result was the light cruiser. This cruiser left von Spee's Far East Squadron in 1914 and sailed alone in the Indian Ocean, attacking ports and communications links, sinking a Russian cruiser, a French destroyer and 16 merchant ships before being surprised and sunk by an Australian cruiser on November 9, 1914. Between August 2 and that day she had thoroughly disrupted trade in the Indian Ocean, and wasted the time of a far larger group of warships hunting for her.

South Carolina *(1910, USA)*
Although finished three and a half years after *Dreadnought*, because of many building delays, *South Carolina* was, in fact, the first battleship designed on the all big gun principle. It was a superior design in some respects, though slower and limited in size for cost reasons.

Kongo *(1913, Japan)*
Japan's first battlecruiser and last major warship to be built abroad (in Britain – her three sisters were built in Japan). By the time that she was completed she was the most powerful battlecruiser in the world. She was rebuilt and modernized twice, in 1929-31 and 1936-37,

because of the Washington Naval Treaty of 1922 which prohibited the construction of new capital ships. In 1941 she was involved in the Japanese invasions in Southeast Asia, and in 1942 participated in the Battle of Midway and operations around the Solomon Islands. Refitted in 1943-44, she took part in the Battle of the Philippine Sea and Leyte Gulf, and was sunk in November 1944 by a US submarine.

Seydlitz *(1914, Germany)*
Germany's fourth battlecruiser and typical of the type used in the First World War. She was present at all major engagements between the British and German fleets including the Battle of Jutland (the only time when the opposing battleships met). She was hit by 21 heavy shells, 2 medium ones and a torpedo but still managed to get back to port with 5400 tonnes (5300 tons) of water in the hull because of her good armor protection and excellent damage control procedures. British battlecruisers, because of a design fault in the turret, tended to explode and sink if the turret was hit by one heavy shell. The *Seydlitz*, with the rest of the battlecruisers of the German High Seas Fleet, was surrendered to the Allies in 1918, and interned at the British naval base at Scapa Flow.

Seydlitz

Queen Elizabeth *(1915, Britain)*
The first battleship to carry a main armament of 380mm (15 in) guns. She served as the flagship of the British fleet from 1917 till 1924, overseeing the surrender of the German fleet at the end of the First World War (1918) which then scuttled itself in order to avoid being handed over to Germany's former enemies. She was rebuilt twice between the First and Second World Wars for the same reason as *Kongo* and saw much service in the Second World War, at the end of 1941, being sunk at Alexandria (Egypt) by Italian frogmen riding self-propelled torpedoes.

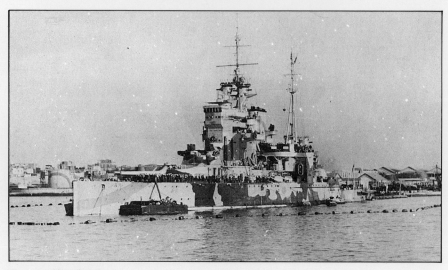

Queen Elizabeth

Petropavlosk *(1915, Russia)*
Last of the Gangut class, Russia's first Dreadnought type battleship in the Baltic Sea. She was part of Russia's attempt to rebuild its fleet after the Russo-Japanese War. She helped keep the much more powerful German fleet away from the capital, St. Petersburg (now Leningrad). Although sailors were some of the main supporters of the 1917 Russian Revolution, the crew of the *Petropavlosk* led a mutiny against the new Communist leadership in 1920. In 1923 it was renamed *Marat*. Despite being sunk by German dive bombers in 1941, in shallow water, the battleship's guns helped to defend Leningrad which was under siege between 1941-44, reverting to the name *Petropavlosk* in 1943.

Furious *(1917, Britain)*
She was designed as a cruiser, but then given two 457mm (18 in) guns as a trial. Two were not enough for any practical use because the gunnery standards of the day demanded at least six and preferably eight guns, firing together to have a reasonable chance of hitting anything because of their inaccuracy. Before she was completed, however, the Battle of Jutland showed a need for a ship which could both carry aircraft and keep up with the fleet. Thus, the front gun was removed and a flight deck put in its place. This meant that she could launch but not land aircraft. So *Furious* went back to dock and had her rear gun removed and a landing deck and a hangar to store the aircraft fitted. But landing was still very difficult because the funnel, and the superstructure, poked up in the middle of the deck, making wind eddies into which the landing aircraft had to fly which was almost impossible. She then had all her superstructure removed. Finally, it was realized that some superstructure (mounted on the side of the ship) was needed to allow the captain to control what was going on, but this was not fitted until 1938. Nonetheless she managed to play a useful part in World War Two, fighting off Norway and running supplies to the island of Malta.

Argus *(1918, Britain)*
Unlike *Furious*, *Argus* had the advantage of being initially designed with a continuous deck. It was the first design which could be easily converted to carry aircraft. She was, however, very small and was mainly used for pilot training during her life.

Petropavlosk

Furious

Hood

Hood *(1920, Britain)*

Too late for the First World War, *Hood* was Britain's last battlecruiser and largest capital ship of her day at 46,950 tonnes (46,200 tons), until she was sunk (the others being limited to 35,570 tonnes (35,000 tons) by the Washington Naval Treaty of 1922). As the fastest and the largest warship of the British fleet, she was the pride of the fleet and her loss, while fighting the *Bismark* in 1941, was a great national shock. However, as a battlecruiser, speed mattered more than protection and she was no match for the much better protected *Bismark*, the new German battleship.

Tennessee *(1920, USA)*

At the end of the First World War, both the USA and Japan had massive shipbuilding programs in operation. If the balance of naval power was to remain constant, Britain, USA and Japan would have to continue building large numbers of capital ships, which they did not need and at great expense, or try and come to agreement limiting shipbuilding. They came to an agreement, the Washington Naval Treaty of 1922, affecting ships all over the world. This limited the number of battleships, battlecruisers and aircraft carriers and also limited the maximum size that these ships could be. *Tennessee* was one of the last ships finished before the Treaty. She was badly damaged at Pearl Harbor (1941) but was repaired and used for bombarding islands prior to US Marine assaults, operating against Tarawa, Kwajalein, Eniwetok, Kavieng, Saipan, Guam, Tinian, Palau, Leyte, Iwo Jima and Okinawa. Placed in reserve in 1945, she was finally scrapped in 1959.

Hosho *(1922, Japan)*

The first purpose built aircraft carrier to be completed (the British *Hermes* was the first to be designed and laid down but was not finished until 1923). She was used mainly for experiments and training, being too small for active duty, though she was active for a short while at the beginning of World War Two.

Lexington *(1927, USA)*

The Washington Treaty meant that several ships under construction had to be abandoned. One way to get around this, however, was to convert some of the battlecruisers, then being built, into large aircraft carriers, the small carriers of Britain (*Argus*), Japan (*Hosho*) and the USA (*Langley*) having given the major navies experience in carrier operations. Thus, the battlecruiser *Lexington* and her sister, *Saratoga* (design based on that of *Hood*) were converted and were the largest carriers until the end of the Second World War. In that war *Lexington* was lost early on in the Battle of Coral Sea in 1942. Her loss, however, prevented the further expansion of captured Japanese territory southward, ending the imminent threat to Australia.

Akagi *(1927, Japan)*

Akagi and her sister *Amagi* were the direct counterparts of *Lexington*. *Amagi*, however, was very seriously damaged in an earthquake and her position was taken over by *Kage*. *Akagi* took part in Pearl Harbor, which crippled the US Pacific fleet at the start of the Pacific War. She was lost at the Battle of Midway in 1942 with three other Japanese carriers. The battle marked the end of the Japanese domination of the Pacific. Japan's strength never recovered as the US strength continued to grow with the mass production of Essex class carriers. Midway also marked the point where everyone had to recognize that the carrier, and not the battleship, was the most important warship.

Lexington

Exeter (1931, Britain)

Further attempts at arms control after the Washington Treaty focused on limiting cruisers. These were restricted, after much argument, to 203mm (8 in) guns and a displacement of 10,170 tonnes (10,000 tons). The major navies, therefore, began building cruisers to these dimensions, including Britain. But with her large empire, Britain felt she needed a great number of cruisers and therefore built *Exeter* and her sister *York* as small and as cheaply as possible but still armed with the minimum number of 203mm (8 in) guns. Smaller cruisers with 152mm (6 in) guns were thereafter built but *Exeter* still had an active if brief war. In 1939 she, with two 152mm (6 in) gun cruisers, stopped the *Graf Spee* (armed with six 280mm (11 in) guns) and forced it to retreat to the South American port of Montevideo where, believing that the British force outside outgunned him, the captain ordered the *Graf Spee* to be scuttled. *Exeter* was very badly damaged in the battle but was repaired and then sent to the Far East. There, at the Battle of Java Sea with Dutch and US ships, she helped to try and stop the Japanese invasion of the Dutch East Indies. The attempt failed and the damaged *Exeter* was sunk, three days later, by heavy cruisers.

Le Fantasque (1931, France)

Throughout the century the French Navy have maintained a moderate but powerful force operating in the coastal seas of the Mediterranean and North Sea. This resulted in some novel ship designs. Among them was a group of ships known as *Contre Torpilleurs*. Smaller than cruisers but larger than destroyers, they were heavily armed, very fast (with speeds over 40 knots) but totally unprotected. Their role was to make very fast sweeps into enemy areas under cover of darkness and return by daybreak. They never had the opportunity to try this in wartime, but, in any event, they would have been very vulnerable to light cruisers.

Mogami (1935, Japan)

One of the consequences of the Washington Naval Treaty and later treaties in the series was to place Japan in a permanent position of inferiority to the USA and Britain. For every five battleships or carriers or cruisers that the US and Britain had, Japan was only allowed to have three. This was called the 5:5:3 ratio. To get round this, Japan used both considerable innovation and they cheated. The Mogami class of cruisers showed both of these tactics. Japan had already built its quota of 203mm (8 in) gunned cruisers. *Mogami* was designed as a 10,170 tonne (10,000 ton) ship (the maximum allowed) but was actually 12,600 tonnes (12,400 tons) heavier. She was fitted with fifteen 155mm (6 in) guns but on mounts which could be rapidly changed to take 200mm (7.9 in) guns if necessary. Thus, creating a 203mm (8 in) gun cruiser in the guise of a 152mm (6 in) gun light cruiser. Despite being over the Treaty weight limit, attempts to keep the weight down showed structural weakness which had to be corrected soon after completion. The difference in power between a 152mm (6 in) large light cruiser and a 203mm (8 in) heavy cruiser was not too great and both the US and Britain were so impressed with the original design of *Mogami* that they produced similar designs, the Brooklyn and Town class, respectively. Indeed, Britain gave up building heavy cruisers altogether. The *Mogami* and her three sisters proved to be very robust ships. After receiving a lot of damage during the Battle of Midway (in which the sister *Mikoma* was sunk) *Mogami* had her two stern turrets removed and replaced with a flight deck for seaplanes, giving it six 200mm (7.9 in) guns and 11 seaplanes. *Mogami* was lost in 1944.

Le Fantasque

Admiral Graf Spee *(1936, Germany)*
Like Japan, Germany resented the Treaty limitations placed upon it. In the peace treaty ending the First World War, Germany was forbidden to build any ship larger than 10,170 tonnes (10,000 tons). Like the Japanese, the Germans used technical skill and cheating to get around this. They created the Deutschland class, of which the *Graf Spee* was the third and last, describing them simply as Armored Ships, though outside Germany they became known as pocket battleships because on a cruiser hull of 12,300 tonnes (12,000 tons) displacement) they placed a battleship-like main armament of six 280mm (11 in) guns. They were faster and so could run away from battleships, while they were more powerfully armed than any cruisers (which were faster than the *Graf Spee*). Only a handful of battlecruisers could really tackle these ships. Their aim was to roam the seas destroying merchant ships and disrupting trade and for this they had diesel engines for long range cruising. The *Graf Spee*, however, was lost in 1939 by a combination of dogged attacks by British and New Zealand cruisers and deception which led the captain to believe that greatly superior forces had been concentrated against him,

that there was no point in further resistance so he scuttled the ship. Although these ships gave Germany a powerful naval force they were not a great success in their intended role. German submarines, U-Boats, were much better at disrupting trade and in 1940 the two remaining ships, *Deutschland* (renamed *Lützow*) and *Admiral Scheer* were reclassified as heavy cruisers and spent a largely inactive war in the Baltic after helping in the conquest of Norway.

De Ruyter *(1936, The Netherlands)*
The Dutch only maintained a small navy, since the Netherlands followed a policy of neutrality. But to protect their East Indies colony (now Indonesia) *De Ruyter* was built as the flagship of the East Indies Squadron. However, the lack of international coordination and the speed of the Japanese advance overwhelmed all the Allies in the Pacific in 1941 and early 1942. *De Ruyter* was sunk at the Battle of Java Sea when an Anglo-Dutch-US force tried to stop the Japanese capture of the East Indies.

Southampton *(1937, Britain)*
This was the first of ten Town class large light cruisers built after Britain was so impressed by the Japanese Mogami class. These formed the

backbone of Britain's cruiser force during the Second World War, being a well balanced design with a powerful armament of twelve 152 mm (6 in) guns, a well organized anti-aircraft defense and reasonable armor protection. Her sister *Belfast*, which took part in the sinking of the German battlecruiser *Scharnhorst*, is now preserved as a museum.

Dunkerque *(1937, France)*
France, concerned by the increasing numbers of heavy cruisers, decided to build warships to counter them. Advances in engine design meant that battleships could be built with the speed of battlecruisers without sacrificing armor protection. Thus, *Dunkerque* had high speed and a main armament of 330mm (13 in) guns. These were mounted in 4-gun turrets forward, with the secondary guns mounted at the stern. This arrangement allowed the ship to be built on a relatively small scale, and thus cheaply. The *Dunkerque* was present at the Battle of Mers el Kebir (1940), when the British, afraid that the French fleet would fall into German hands after the defeat of France, asked the French to disarm and surrender their ships. When they refused, the British attacked, badly damaging the *Dunkerque*.

Admiral Graf Spee

Brooklyn *(1938, USA)*
This, and the follow-on class, Cleveland, formed the backbone of the US fleet's cruiser force during the Second World War, a total of 34 of the two classes being built. They were based on the Mogami large light cruiser concept. Nine of the Cleveland class were converted to light aircraft carriers (Independence class) to quickly increase the number of aircraft carriers available. Several were converted to carry guided missiles after the war and others were sold off to foreign navies, including the USS *Phoenix*, which, renamed by her owner, Argentina, as the *General Belgrano*, took part in the Falklands War, of 1982.

Ark Royal (1938, Britain)

After the experience gained with the initial carriers, Britain, in 1930, set about planning a force of five carriers, capable of operating a total of 360 aircraft. Several years lapsed until the money for the first of these, *Ark Royal*, was found. Along with its US counterpart, the Yorktown class, it was the first purpose-built large carrier incorporating all the experience gained earlier. She had a brief but active career, being Britain's only modern carrier at the start of the Second World War. She helped search for the *Graf Spee* in 1939, fought off Norway, attacked the French fleet at Mers el Kebir (one of its planes torpedoing *Dunkerque*), helped to develop the idea of the carrier battle group when stationed at Gibraltar in "Force H," and fought against the Italians in 1940. In 1941 she operated in the Mediterranean, searched for a group of German warships, including *Scharnhorst*, which had been sent to disrupt trade, in the Atlantic, and hunted, found and crippled the German battleship *Bismark*, the pride of the German Navy, who was in the Atlantic on another trade disruption mission. She was finally sunk in November 1941.

Scharnhorst (1939, Germany)

The building of *Dunkerque* made the pocket battleship idea obsolete, and the German response was *Scharnhorst* and her sister *Gneisenau*. They were large ships but the lack of design skill in Germany (which had not built a major ship in over 15 years) showed. They were under-protected, under-gunned, with 280mm (11 in) guns, though 380mm (15 in) guns were intended to be fitted once the turret had been designed, while the engines were unreliable. Nonetheless, their existence worried the British fleet, and their threat of sorties to Atlantic trade tied down large numbers of British warships. Their greatest feat was the "Channel Dash," when both sisters left the French port of Brest and ran at full speed through the Channel to reach

Ark Royal

the Baltic bases for refit and repairs, leaving a surprised British fleet unable to react quickly enough. The *Scharnhorst* was finally sunk in the battle of North Cape, when she was caught by a powerful British task force while attempting to stop convoys reaching Russia.

Richelieu (1940, France)

After the success of *Dunkerque*, the French decided that it was time to rebuild their aging battle fleet, so they built the *Richelieu* and her sister *Jean Bart*. She was built to the same pattern as *Dunkerque*, with all her main guns forward. But the invention of more powerful engines allowed *Richelieu* to be given a full armor protection. Thus she had battlecruiser speed and the protection of a battleship. *Richelieu* was all but finished by the time Germany conquered France and, just ahead of the advancing Germans, the battleship sailed to Dakar in West Africa. There she repelled an attempt to capture the colony by the Free French under General de Gaulle. In 1943 she joined the Allies and was taken to the US to be finally completed, after which she operated in the Pacific with the British Pacific Fleet off the Dutch East Indies. After the Second World War, the *Richelieu* continued to serve with the French Navy until placed in reserve in 1956 and scrapped in 1968.

Scharnhorst

Bismark *(1940, Germany)*

This ship and her sister, *Tirpitz*, attracted a great deal of attention in the Second World War. The British Navy repeatedly tried to destroy them because of the threat they posed to the convoys between North America and Britain and between Britain and Russia. The design, while powerful and larger than any British battleship, still suffered from the German's lack of design experience, because they were not allowed to build battleships after the First World War. In particular, her armor used an inferior grade of steel compared to US and British ships, and she was laid out in a way which made the *Bismark* very hard to sink. But, unfortunately she was sunk on her first mission into the North Atlantic, after sinking the battle cruiser *Hood*. She was immobilized by torpedoes, dropped from aircraft from *Ark Royal*, and overwhelmed by a group of battleships and cruisers.

Vittorio Veneto *(1940, Italy)*

The *Vittorio Veneto* was Italy's most modern class of battleship in the Second World War. She almost suffered the same fate as *Bismark* when she was hit by aircraft, from the carrier *Formidable*, at the Battle of Cape Matapan when her escorting cruisers were caught and destroyed by the British battleships. She surrendered with the Italian fleet in 1943 after Italy's surrender and sailed to the British port of Malta.

Bismark

Yamato *(1941, Japan)*

Completed a few days after Japan's entry into the Second World War with the devastating attack on the US Pacific Fleet at Pearl Harbor she and her sister *Musashi* were the largest and most powerful battleships ever built. Ironically, she was built only in time to witness the end of the battleship era, and the beginning of the aircraft carrier era. So she spent most of her time escorting the carriers. Her end came in 1945. As the US invaded the island of Okinawa, *Yamato* was sent on a suicide mission to disrupt the landings. With only enough fuel to get to the island, she never reached her target, as she was overwhelmed and sunk by massed air attacks from US carriers.

Fletcher *(1942, USA)*

Many destroyers were needed to protect the carriers and the convoys across the vast distances of the Pacific. Thus the US industry began mass-producing them. 181 Fletcher, and improved Fletcher, class destroyers were built in a four year period (1942-45), with another 98 of the successor class, the Gearing, being built between 1945 and 1951. Some are still in service in smaller navies, having received a modernization known as FRAM (Fleet Rehabilitation And Modernization).

Essex *(1942, USA)*

As destroyers were mass-produced, so were the carriers. 24 Essex class fleet carriers were built in the Second World War, and became the cornerstone of the US naval power in the 1940s and 50s. Today, *Lexington* (of this class) is still in service. Now immobilized, her flight deck is used for naval pilots making their first carrier take offs and landings.

Yamato

Fletcher

Casablanca (1942, USA)

While the main Task Forces used the Essex class carriers to control the seas, there was still a great need for carriers to provide air cover for small groups of warships, convoys and landing operations. The US thus adopted a British idea, the escort carrier, and used its industrial might to build over 50 of the Casablanca class alone. The escort carrier was built on a merchant ship hull and was small, cheap and only took a year to build.

Iowa (1943, USA)

After *Yamato*, these were the most powerful battleships ever built. The four ships of this class were used in the Second World War escorting the carriers. After that war, they were used for shore bombardment in the Korean War of the early 1950s, and then placed in reserve. Destroyers and cruisers with guided missiles had, by then, become better escorts for the carriers. The sister ship, *New Jersey*, was brought out of reserve during the Vietnam war in the late 1960s, again to provide support for the land force. She was then again placed in reserve, as it was thought that the day of the battleship was finally over and that they would never again see active service. However, the development of long range cruise missiles in the 1970s led to the suggestion that the four Iowas would make excellent platforms for these weapons. They were very well protected, and cheap to bring back to service in comparison to building new vessels. In addition,

the ship's 460mm (18 in) main guns would be useful in marine landings. So, after years of retirement, the four are now being modernized and brought back to service. *New Jersey* and *Iowa* are already in service with their sisters, *Missouri* and *Wisconsin*, following soon. It is planned that they will form the center of a Surface Act Group, with escorting cruisers and destroyers. They will have less important missions, freeing the Carrier Battle Groups for more important tasks.

Taiho (1944, Japan)

As the US mass-produced the Essex class, the Japanese did their best to keep up, but never had the same industrial resources. *Taiho* was the best, most balanced carrier design that Japan produced, combining all of Japan's carrier building experience from the lessons of the first half of the Second World War. Nonetheless, she was the only one of her class; the follow-on ships were cancelled in favor of simpler ships which could be built faster. But, by the time *Taiho* had been completed, there were not enough trained naval pilots to operate her aircraft. Japan did not have the resources for a massive pilot training scheme, and to keep up the correct number of pilots; the training hours were repeatedly cut back to only a few hours. She was sunk by a submarine during working up trials, which is when the crew become familiar with a new ship. The crew was ineffective and *Taiho* sank.

Sverdlov (1952, Russia)

After the Second World War, Stalin, the Soviet leader, decided that he would have a great navy to equal the naval might of the US and Britain. A vast navel program was, therefore, started. The planned fleet, however, did not take account of the experiences of the Second World War. Large numbers of destroyers, submarines and cruisers, such as the Sverdlov class, were built. Many of these remain in service today, though in declining numbers. Two of this class have been converted to command ships for the Black Sea and Pacific fleets. Another was used for trials with an defense missile system which was unsuccessful. Nine others remain, but are either in reserve or used only for training.

Ark Royal (1955, Britain)

Named after the carrier lost in World War Two, this new carrier began construction in 1942. Its completion, however, was delayed by the end of the War and the need to adapt her for jet aircraft operations. This included the new inventions of the steam catapult to launch the aircraft, and the angled flight deck. These allowed aircraft to be landed and launched at the same time. *Ark Royal* also incorporated the idea of aircraft lifts, mounted on the side of the ship. This allowed the space on the flight deck to be used better. She remained as Britain's most powerful warship until the late 1970s.

Iowa

Ark Royal

Whitby *(1956, Britain)*

After the Second World War, Britain and the US faced a big problem. Advances in submarine design meant that the hundreds of anti-submarine escorts built during the war, were useless. To overcome this, some of the wartime destroyers, which were fast enough to catch the new submarines, were, as a temporary measure converted to anti-submarine frigates. But what was really needed was a new anti-submarine frigate design. In Britain this became the Whitby (Type 12) class. They were excellent ships, particularly in the design of their hull, which allowed operations in the most difficult sea conditions. They became the basis of the succeeding Rothesay and Leander class, many of which still remain in service, in Britain and other navies.

Long Beach *(1961, USA)*

The USS *Long Beach* was the first nuclear powered surface warship. She was designed as a cruiser to escort the new nuclear powered aircraft carriers. The initial idea was to have a totally nuclear powered Carrier Battle Group which could operate independently for several months at sea without refueling or any external assistance from either shore bases or replenishment ships. However, putting nuclear power into cruisers has proved to be very expensive and today the US still operates twice as many conventionally powered cruisers as it does nuclear powered ones.

Kynda *(1962, Russia)*

When Stalin died, the direction of the Soviet Navy changed dramatically. Hundreds of ships were cancelled from Stalin's program, and a new fleet, based on missiles instead of guns, was designed. A few of Stalin's ships were converted to missile carriers, as a temporary measure, but the first product of this new plan were the four Kynda class guided missile cruisers. They were armed with 16 long range surface-to-surface missiles, (in eight launchers with one reload each) and an air defense missile system. Their mission was to try to sink the carrier before they were sunk by the carrier's aircraft.

Moskva *(1967, Russia)*

The *Moskva* was completed in 1967 and was called an anti-submarine cruiser. The West have termed the *Moskva*, and her class, as helicopter carriers, as she was modified after completion to test Vertical Landing and Take Off aircraft. She now carries a complement of 14 helicopters. She was designed as the first Soviet ship to take aircraft, and to attempt to counter the threat of submarines carrying the Polaris missile. This role is now redundant as the new submarine-launched ballistic missiles have a longer range than the older Polaris missile. As a result, submarines do not need to go so close to land to launch their missiles, and as *Moskva* has no aircraft complement, she is forced to stay near aircraft bases on land for protection.

Kiev *(1970, Russia)*

The Kiev class of ships were the first Soviet vessels to operate aircraft other than helicopters. The design was thought to be relatively unsuccessful, but in operations she has proved herself to be a good ship to handle, as well as providing a capability in reconnaissance, ground attack and fighter cover. The *Kiev* is the largest vessel that the Russians have built to date, and she is deployed in the Northern Fleet, above the Arctic Circle, and in the Pacific.

Spruance *(1975, USA)*

This is the largest and one of the most controversial destroyer classes since the end of the Second World War. The 31 members of the class, built between 1975 and 1983, were criticized for being too large, too expensive and under-armed. These were the first destroyers since the late 1950s without a major air defense missile system. However, Spruance's main role is anti-submarine warfare and in this it has proved excellent. Much of the expense and size of the destroyer (8,170 tonnes (8,040 tons) full load), is taken up with measures to make the ships especially quiet when listening for enemy submarines. The basic design of the ship has also proved very flexible. The Kidd class destroyers and the Ticonderoga class cruisers use the same basic hull and engines.

Spruance

Long Beach

Oliver Hazard Perry *(1977, USA)*

There are 61 vessels, the *Oliver Hazard Perry* and her sister ships, in the Oliver Hazard Perry class and about half of these are already in service in the US Navy. She is a guided missile frigate and carries a complement of helicopters. *Oliver Hazard Perry* has been fitted with a new modification, a Recovery, Assistance, Securing and Traversing System (RAST) which permits the launching and recovery of aircraft in very heavy seas, an operation that is very difficult. The class was a relatively cheap ship to build, especially designed for the US Navy who wanted large numbers of vessels – it was too expensive to build large numbers of more fully armed ships such as the Spruance and Ticonderoga. Her design gave her the role of escorting rather than the harder missions such as protecting the carrier.

Oliver Hazard Perry

Bal'zam *(1980, Russia)*

The *Bal'zam* is the largest of the Soviet fleet's intelligence gathering vessels. These vessels collect electronic and photographic information on the NATO warships, their radar systems, tactics and so on. The *Bal'zam* or her sister ships, can be seen with most major task groups and they are usually present at almost all NATO exercises. The Soviet fleet relies very heavily on these intelligence gathering vessels as it does not have a world-wide network of electronic monitoring stations on land.

Kirov *(1980, Russia)*

This is the largest surface warship in the world, which is not a carrier or one of the four old Iowa class battleships. She is probably the world's most powerful surface warship except for the carrier. Her main weapons are the long range surface-to-surface missiles, but she also carries two air defense missile systems, two gun systems, an anti-submarine missile system, anti-submarine torpedoes and anti-submarine rocket launchers. She also has three or more helicopters for missile targeting and anti-submarine warfare.

Principe de Asturias *(1986, Spain)*

There has been a great deal of argument about the wisdom of building new 92,000 tonne (90,000 ton) supercarriers. Some claim that the carrier is too vulnerable to attack, since it is the principal target to other navies. Others argue that the cost of the carrier is so great that too few could be built to fulfil all the missions assigned to them. In response to these critics, a small carrier design was prepared. Known as the Sea Control Ship, it was designed to be small enough to undertake secondary missions on which the supercarriers would be wasted. Because it was felt that these ships would take money away from the big carriers (rather than supplementing them, as was intended) they were never built in the US. However, smaller navies with a need for smaller carriers were interested. Spain, with only a small carrier dating from the Second World War, was allowed to use the US design, which has been modified with the British ''Ski-Jump'' runway to allow V/STOL aircraft to take off with a greater payload than if they took off vertically. She will enter service in June 1986.

Bal'zam

Kirov

Surface Warships in Service Today

Number of Ships in Service and *name of class after 1960*

Country (Major navies only)	Aircraft carriers	Cruisers	Destroyers	Frigate		Fast Attack Craft	Mine Counter Measures	Amphib. Assault Ships
Argentina	1		7: Meko Type 360; Type 42	4: Type A 69; Meko 140 Type	7	4	6	1
Australia			3: Perth	10: FFG7; River			1	1
Belgium				4: Wielingen			28	
Brazil	1		12	6: Niteroi	16		6	2
Canada			4: DD280	16: Annapolis; Mackenzie				
Chile			6: Almirante	2: Leander	3	6		3
China			18: Luta	23: Kiang Hu; Kiang Nan; Kiang Tung	14	817	104	44
Denmark				10: Peder Skram; Niels Juel; Hvidbjornen		16	6	
Egypt			5	3		59	12	3
France	3: △ Clemanceau	2	17: Type C 70; Suffren; Type F 67; Type T 56	26: Commandant Riviere; Type A 69		5	23	2
Germany (West)			7: Modified Charles F. Adams; Hamburg	8: Type 122; Koln	6	40	59	
Greece			14	6		24	15	
India	1	1	3	25: Leander	3	16	13	
Italy	2 △	2: Andrea Doria	4: Audace; Impavido	15: Maestrale; Lupo Alpino; Bergamini	8	4	30	
Japan			34: Shirane; Haruna; Tachikaze; Takasuki; Yamagumo; Minegumo	18: DE 227; Ishikari Chikugo; Isuzu		5	36	
South Korea			11	8	10	40	8	
Netherlands			2: Tromp	16: Kortenaer; van Speijk			21	
Norway				5: Oslo	2	47	10	
Pakistan		1	7			20	3	
Peru		1	10	3: Modified Lupo				
Portugal				17: Commandante Joao Belo; Amirante Pereira da Silva; Joao Continho			4	
Spain	1		11: Roger de Lauria	15: FFG7; F30; Andaz; Baleares	5		12	2
Taiwan			26	10	4	32	22	
Turkey			13	4: Berk		20	34	
United Kingdom	3 △		12: Broadsword; Sheffield	44: Amazon; Leander; Tribal; Rothesay			41	2
USSR and Warsaw Pact	6: △ Kiev; Moskva	41: Kirov □; Kara; Slava; Kynda; Kresta; Kresta I	73: Kashin; Modified Kashin; Kanin; Udaloy; Sovremneny	199: Krivak; Krivak II; Koni; Mirka; Mirka I	78	353	542	2
United States	4: □ Nimitz 14: Enterprise; Kitty Hawk; John F. Kennedy	9: □ Virginia; Truxtun; California; Bainbridge; Long Beach 28: Ticonderoga; Belknap; Lealay	69: Kidd; Charles F. Adams; Coontz; Spruance	99: Oliver Hazard Perry; Brooke; Knox; Garcia; Glover; Bronstein		6	21	30

△ – Small carrier operating only V/STOL aircraft and helicopters
□ – Nuclear-powered vessels

All figures are approximate

Ships are normally built in groups called classes – generally named after the first ship completed.

Glossary

Amphibious assault ship A vessel specially designed to land attacking soldiers on to a hostile coastline.

Amphibious warfare Military activity, involving the landing of attacking forces, either directly or by means of landing craft or helicopters, on to a hostile coastline.

Antenna Electronic mast/or aerial, positioned above the ship, for both transmitting and receiving radio and radar signals.

Armament Weapons and the ammunition that arm a warship.

Battery A group of weapons (normally of the same type) which fire simultaneously.

Battleship An armored ship, mounting heavy guns. The most important type of warship until the development of the aircraft carrier.

Bow The front end of the ship.

Bridge The structure which is raised high off the deck, from where the ship is navigated, or in the case of a flagship, a squadron is directed.

Caliber The internal diameter of a gun.

Chaff Material, normally metallic, which is used to confuse the signals from, and to, radar.

Class The term describing a number of vessels that are all alike in design and construction.

Convoy An organized body of merchant ships and/or naval auxiliary vessels, sailing under the protection of warships.

Corvette An ocean-going warship that is slightly smaller than a frigate. It has a displacement of 1524 tonnes (1500 tons) to 4070 tonnes (4000 tons).

Cruiser A large, surface gun- or missile-armed warship, derived from the original concept of a long-range ship, independent of shore support for protracted periods, while protecting trade routes and convoys.

Data base A computer filing system, where the computer stores all its information which it consults when needed.

Deployment Assigning ships or forces to a specific area, or to a specific job.

Destroyer Medium-sized, high-speed warship with a primary role of supporting strike and amphibious forces. It is very similar to a frigate but more powerful, with a displacement of between 4070 tonnes (4000 tons) and 8130 tonnes (8000 tons).

Displacement The measure of the weight of a vessel. It is termed displacement to make the difference from the tonnage capacity that a ship can carry.

Floating dock A floating structure consisting of two walls standing on pontoon tanks, which can be flooded to receive ships and then pumped out again so that the pontoon deck and the ship are dry. This enables repairs to be carried out "below the water level."

Frigate A medium-sized warship, of moderate to high speed, with a primary role of escort and independent deployment. It has a displacement of between 1524 tonnes (1500 tons) and 4070 tonnes (4000 tons).

Hangar A large compartment in which aircraft are stowed, serviced and repaired.

Hovercraft A vessel that rests on a highly pressurized cushion of air. It is similar to the hydrofoil as it skims over the surface of the water.

Hull The main body of the vessel, excluding the superstructure, masts, funnels, etc.

Hydrofoil A very fast vessel which is supported on legs, ending in foils, thus keeping the hull of the vessel clear of the water at high speeds. The foils skim over the water and therefore little drag is created to slow it down.

Jamming A term that describes the deliberate confusion of enemy radar, radio or sonar signals.

Knot A measurement of ships' speeds. A knot is one nautical mile per hour. A nautical mile is 1.85km (1.15 miles).

Optical sensor A sensor that can detect sightings over a very long distance.

Patrol boat A term to describe small, fast craft. They are usually deployed either inshore, in restricted waters or in rivers where the warship is too large to maneuver.

Port 1. A naval term meaning the left-hand side of the ship. 2. Another word for a harbor.

Radar Electronic ranging device which gives a visual display in plan of the direction in which something, such as an aircraft, is traveling. It also gives a close approximation of bearing, or how close the object is.

Reactors Nuclear reactors. The name for the machinery where the atoms react with one another, which ultimately creates nuclear energy.

Sensor A device, usually electronic, for extending the natural senses of sight and hearing – sonar and radar.

Starboard A naval term meaning the right-hand side of the ship.

Stern The back end of the ship.

Supply ship A small vessel that is not designed to fight in battle, but to support and resupply those that do.

Tugs Small vessels with a very high power-weight ratio, primarily designed for towing, but also used to assist in the berthing and unberthing of ships.

Warship A term to describe modern fighting vessels.

Index

PRINTED IN BELGIUM BY
proost
INTERNATIONAL BOOK PRODUCTION